THE NO NONSENSE GUIDE TO PENDULUMS

Demystifying Pendulum Dowsing and Healing for New and Advanced Practitioners

RENU ARORA

Copyright © 2025

All rights are reserved, and no part of this publication may be reproduced, distributed, or transmitted in any manner, whether through photocopying, recording, or any other electronic or mechanical methods, without the explicit prior written permission of the publisher. This restriction applies to any form or means of reproduction or distribution.

Exceptions to this rule include brief quotations that may be incorporated into critical reviews, as well as certain other noncommercial uses that are allowed by copyright law. Any such usage must adhere to the specified conditions and permissions outlined by the copyright holder.

Book Design by HMDPublishing.com

*To Simone, Gabriel, and Aubrey,
for your unwavering love and support.*

*And to Brian, for encouraging me to
write this book in the first place.*

CONTENTS

FOREWORD _____ 5
INTRODUCTION _____ 7

01. WHERE IT ALL BEGAN _____ 10
02. MY INTRODUCTION TO PENDULUMS _____ 18
03. WHAT CAN BE USED AS A PENDULUM? _____ 22
04. WHY WOULD YOU WANT TO USE
    A PENDULUM, ANYWAY? _____ 25
05. THE BODY PENDULUM _____ 28
06. HOW TO USE A PENDULUM _____ 30
07. HOW TO PROGRAM A PENDULUM _____ 35
08. HOW TO GET ANSWERS THAT ARE
    BOTH FAST AND ACCURATE _____ 38
09. PENDULUMS CAN ANSWER MORE THAN YES AND NO _____ 45
10. PRO-TIP FOR PROGRAMMING YOUR PENDULUM _____ 49
11. CONNECTING WITH...WHAT? _____ 51
12. WHAT TO ASK, AND NOT TO ASK _____ 54
13. DOES IT MATTER WHAT YOUR PENDULUM IS MADE OF? ___ 57
14. BUYING A PENDULUM _____ 61
15. ACCLIMATING TO YOUR PENDULUM _____ 64
16. HEALING WITH A PENDULUM _____ 67
17. TAKING CARE OF YOUR PENDULUM _____ 72
18. A PENDULUM SESSION – FROM START TO FINISH _____ 75
19. WHEN YOUR PENDULUM DOES "WEIRD STUFF" _____ 79
20. SOME FINAL WORDS _____ 82

APPENDIX _____ 84
ABOUT THE AUTHOR _____ 90

FOREWORD

There are myriad books on the market about hypnosis, hypnotherapy, alternative medicine, mind-body work, and the subconscious mind.

Many books are written about how to create change, communicate with the subconscious mind, and manifest healing of the mind, the body and the soul.

I'm a retired physician and hypnotherapist with over fifty years of experience practicing hypnotherapy, and I've read numerous books on all the aspects of creating meaningful change. I thought I read all the important books on the subconscious mind, and conscious subconscious communication. I couldn't imagine anything new and exciting about the topic.

Then Renu sent me a draft of this book, and my opinion was changed by three hundred and sixty degrees.

Here is an incredible addition that will long be a classic, not just on the topic of communication with the subconscious mind, but an in-depth description of how change happens, what is the art and science of the change process, and how to accomplish it with ease.

Renu is a most accomplished healer and teacher. Her students and clients easily learn to manifest powerful new experiences in their lives and frequently gain more than they thought they would accomplish in their connection with her. She is a master at her craft with a gentle, caring approach, which she created based on her deeply held desire to contribute and improve the lives of those fortunate enough to experience her therapy.

This book needs to be in the libraries of new and experienced therapists of all styles. I heartily recommend it.

Dr. Brian Pound

MB BS LRCP MRCS LMCC

Physician & Hypnotherapist

Author of seven books on the subject of hypnosis & hypnotherapy, guest speaker and teacher.

CHAPTER 1:
WHERE IT ALL BEGAN

While I now have complete faith that a little "weight on a string" can provide insight into the goings on of the entire spiritual realm, I certainly didn't start off that way!

When I started off on this journey, I was about as skeptical as they come. As a thorough believer in science (with a Bachelor of Science in Biochemistry from McGill University and over a decade spent as a registered dietitian), a daughter to a *very vocal* atheist father (the phrase "Man created God" was a regular refrain when talk of religion was mentioned in my household), and lacking any obvious intuitive or spiritual gifts, I was about the last person one would expect to feel any connection to spirituality.

To be fair, though, I was humble enough to recognize that science is always evolving. As we develop more sophisticated methods of experimentation and manipulation of the natural world, we must adapt accordingly. Scientists don't know everything—it's hubris to think they do. That's why I've always kept an open mind. I didn't believe everything I was told, but I also didn't dismiss things out of hand. I've always believed that I would rather know the truth than be right. If you could book, you'll find links to very short YouTube videos I've created, especially for my visual learners, who better see what I'm describing than read it. The full collection of videos can also be accessed at: bit.ly/NoNonsensePendulums (The link is case sensitive, so type it exactly as written.)

I hope you're ready, because you're about to immerse yourself into learning the most remarkable skill you will ever learn!

Before I dive into everything you want to know about pendulums, let me give you a quick background about myself. I was introduced to the world of energy work in early 2013, and by November 2015, I had made energy healing my full-time profession using my own healing modality called the Accelerated Release Technique™.

My work is with the subconscious mind. I believe, without a shadow of a doubt, that every single one of the challenges we currently face in our lives is there for a reason. Absolutely nothing is random. These challenges are signals from your subconscious that some healing needs to happen. Whether the healing is for trauma from this lifetime or a past lifetime, unprocessed ancestral trauma passed down through generations, or vicarious experiences we have taken on behalf of someone else, it makes no difference. With the right tool, you can unlock all the answers, solve all the mysteries, and overcome every challenge—so you can finally be the master of your own life, creating it to be precisely what you want.

Your pendulum can be that tool.

Armed with only my pendulum and my list of questions, I've been able to help people eliminate issues of all kinds. Emotional, mental, and physical issues across the spectrum: fears and phobias, anxiety, depression, anger, grief, self-doubt, limiting beliefs, relationship problems, chronic pains, food allergies, environmental intolerances, sleeping difficulties, hair loss, eczema, and the list goes on.

How I do all of that is the topic for another book. But none of it would have been possible without my skills with a pendulum. Anyone can develop a skill with a little knowledge and a lot of practice.

They say a picture is worth a thousand words. Well, a video must be worth about a million of them! Throughout this

INTRODUCTION

I would like to preface this book with one fact: I have had only two "lessons" in pendulum use. I'll discuss them both in detail within the following pages, but I share this because I want you to know that I went into this without any biases. There were no rules. Nobody told me what a pendulum could or couldn't be used for, so I was open to the possibilities. Only after I had been using it for several years did I discover I was doing things differently from what conventional wisdom would say. So please don't be surprised if I make a claim that doesn't fit what you think you know. Go ahead and give it a try anyway.

Why am I writing this book? Whenever I look at discussion boards for pendulum usage, I see that there seem to be twelve different answers to every question. If I didn't have enough faith in my own abilities, it would be enough to make me question if *I* was doing something wrong! You see, most dowsers are either doing what someone else told them to do or what simply feels "right" to them.

What are the "must dos"? What are simply "could dos"? And what are people doing that is actually a waste of time, but they just don't know better? I wanted to provide a guide that would cut through the confusion, giving you the straight goods on what is verified as important and what you can skip altogether.

prove something to me, I would be willing to change what I believe.

And so, when I was introduced to "muscle testing," it turned my world on its head!

Muscle testing is a bridge connecting the spiritual and physical worlds.

I describe in detail how to muscle test in my book, *The Energy Healing Bible*, in my online course, *Connecting to Your Subconscious without Hypnosis*, and there are plenty of descriptions available on the internet, so I won't describe the process here. In a nutshell, muscle testing is a way to use the body to get answers directly from the subconscious mind.

You can muscle test yourself or others and use large muscles (like the arm) or small muscles (like the fingers) to receive answers.

Armed with these instructions, the subconscious can be used to get a remarkable amount of information. Muscle testing is a gateway to connecting to your own intuition.

And like I said, it opened my eyes to an entire world I didn't know existed.

My first real encounter with muscle testing—and energy healing, in a way—was in January 2013, in the office of Robert Tomilson at the Institute of National Health Technologies in Oakville, Ontario. He is the co-founder of BIE (Bioenergetic Intolerance Elimination), and I had met a practitioner of that modality a few days earlier. She had piqued my curiosity, so I made an appointment with Robert to learn about it directly from the source.

He told me a fascinating tale: everything is energy, vibrating at its own frequency, and when we have an intolerance or adverse reaction to something (a food, for example), it is because our body doesn't recognize that particular frequency. It's as though the frequency is not listed in our own personal database. As a result, our body doesn't know how to process it properly and will attempt to get rid of it in any way it can.

For example, a food that is "unrecognized" is unable to be properly digested and excreted through the normal process; instead, the body will use alternate methods to rid itself of the foreign substance - namely the kidneys, the colon, the respiratory system, or the skin.

If it's the kidneys, the body will just try to "pee it out," and the individual will need to make frequent trips to the bathroom soon after consuming the offending food.

When the colon is involved, you may experience constipation or diarrhea, gas or bloating with the food.

Foods that affect the respiratory system trigger congestion, sneezing, and wheezing. This conversation was back when I was a dietitian, so when told of this, I immediately recollected one client who told me she would always sneeze multiple times whenever she would drink coffee. It seemed strange to us both at the time, but Robert's explanation gave me something to think about.

Finally, when the skin is involved, one may experience rashes, hives, or eczema as the body tries to eliminate the food that way.

He then went on to tell me that he had developed a technique to essentially "teach" the body to recognize the missing frequencies using a specially developed machine, after which the intolerance would disappear.

That's when I did a mental eye-roll.

This is NOT how allergies worked, my mind reminded me. We react to food because our bodies have mistakenly created antibodies for it, so when it is consumed, the substance and the antibody combine to form a lock-and-key interaction that triggers the allergic response. Allergies are a *physical response* to a *physical substance*.

But I wasn't going to be rude and walk out, so I continued to listen patiently.

He said he wanted to show me how it worked.

He asked me if there was anything I reacted to.

Well, that was unexpected! I told him that I had an intolerance to soy and that eating it would give me gas and bloating.

He disappeared into another room for a moment and returned with a small vial, about the size of a spice jar, filled with a mixture of soybeans and soy flour. He told me he was going to "muscle test" me. He asked me to squeeze my thumb and ring finger together and resist while he tried to pull them apart. I was quite strong, so he had to use a lot of force to open my fingers, and even then, only slightly.

He then told me he had to calibrate - to make sure that he could test me properly. He asked me to put my left hand on my head, palm down, as he pulled apart the fingers on my right hand again. This time, my fingers didn't move. I wasn't convinced he was really trying...he had been able to open my fingers at least a little bit just a moment ago.

Then he had me flip my left hand over, so my palm would be up, while he did the test again. This time, my fingers had absolutely no strength at all! It was like all the energy had been drained from my arm. How could that be? I made him do it again.

And again, with my palm facing down, my fingers were strong. With palm up, as weak as a kitten.

Before we could go on, I needed an explanation.

He shared that we have energy fields going through and around us. Positive energy goes up out the top of our heads, and negative energy returns in the palms of our hands and the soles of our feet. Like the terminals of a battery.

The first test was to figure out how strong I was, and determine for himself how much strength he needed to apply in order to pull my fingers apart just a little bit. He knew to use the same amount of strength each time.

With that in mind, he had me put my hand on top of my head, palm down. Doing that closed the circuit. The positive energy coming out of my head was returning back into the palm of my hand, and as a result, I was holding energy in my body - none was escaping. In that situation, I suddenly had more energy - more strength - and Rob's strength, which was only just enough to pull my fingers apart earlier, was not enough to pull my stronger fingers apart.

When I had my palm faced up, the opposite occurred. The *back* of the hand is another place for positive energy to be emitted. So the back of my hand against the top of my head is positive against positive; and just like when you flip one magnet when two magnets had been previously stuck together, they now repel each other. The effect was that I didn't just break the closed circuit from previously, but I was essentially pushing my energy to the floor, making myself weaker than in my original state. So when Rob tested me in this situation, my weakened state meant that my finger strength felt non-existent.

This was tangible proof that we have energy fields. That our energy extends beyond the surface of the skin - going through and around our body.

My mind started reeling with the implications.

Satisfied that I was appropriately calibrated and that his tests would yield accurate results, Rob then had me take the vial of soy in the hand not being tested and hold it to the forearm of the hand being tested. Then he asked me to resist the pull again. And my fingers were weak. Just like when I had that hand, held palm up, on my head earlier. What?? I made him do it again. Without the vial, Rob could pull my fingers apart only slightly; with the vial, my strength disappeared. He explained how there was a repulsion of energy along my arm when the soy was nearby, as though the energy had moved away to get away from the soy.

Then he did something I'll never forget. He told me to hold the vial of soy *on my left leg*. He was testing the muscles using my right hand, so this time when he asked me to resist, my muscles felt *super strong*. What the heck? Just as there had been an energy repulsion on my arm when the soy was held there, the same occurred with my left leg; only this time, the energy being pushed away from my leg moved towards my arm!

And then, before I could really process all of that, he whisked the vial of soy onto his little machine and had me get comfortable for my very first BIE session. The machine was essentially a metal plate whose function was to pick up all the frequencies of the vials placed upon it, and pulse those frequencies through a small rod that was touched to various parts of my body - mainly on the face and feet - "teaching" my body the frequency of soy through this current running through my body.

In less than 15 minutes, we were done. Rob then had me muscle test the soy vial again. After bringing it to my forearm this time, my muscles felt as strong as iron. My fingers didn't budge. With a big smile on Rob's face, he said, "you're done now."

"You're telling me I can eat soy now?"

"Yes," he replied.

And that was it. He said my body was able to recognize soy now and that I wouldn't react to it anymore.

Still skeptical, because that's *just NOT how allergies work*, I resolved that I would at least have to give it a try to see for myself. A couple of days later I consumed a rather large quantity of soy one evening (my reaction was always felt the following day, so I needed to have enough to be absolutely certain that there would be a noticeable reaction soon enough not to confuse it with anything else) and went to bed. When I woke up, I felt absolutely nothing. Not a twinge. I was gobsmacked! "The reaction is just delayed," I told myself. I watched the clock all day, expecting my insides to rise up and explode at any moment, but the gas and bloating never came.

And now I had to re-evaluate everything I thought I knew about how the world worked.

We have energy fields! Chi? Auras? Chakras? *Real*???

Our bodies respond to the *energy frequency* of the things around us? And there are ways to heal ourselves through energy?

Within the next 24 hours, I reached out to Rob and made plans to become a BIE practitioner. It wasn't long before I picked up another bombshell during my training.

The subconscious is extremely amenable to commands. It is always listening. And it *wants* to communicate with us. The commands when muscle testing are essentially "when faced with something true, or beneficial, make the muscles stronger" and "when faced with something untrue or detrimental, make the muscles weaker."

Using muscle testing, you can use "yes" and "no" questions to get answers directly from your subconscious. And with a handful of resources and some experience with asking good questions, one can gain powerful insights into exactly what makes us tick!

Key takeaways:

Muscle testing is the bridge between the physical world and the spiritual one. It can be used to prove the existence of energy fields and the fact that our responses to the world are not the result of physical interactions, but energetic ones. And when we know how to change our energy, we can heal.

CHAPTER 2:
MY INTRODUCTION TO PENDULUMS

Once I learned that you could use muscle testing to connect with the subconscious, it wasn't long before I learned techniques to connect our present struggles to the emotional baggage we are carrying from unresolved, or unhealed, life experiences.

Simultaneously, I picked up techniques to heal that emotional baggage.

As I said in the last chapter, the subconscious *wants* to communicate with us. **All** of the challenges we face - emotional, mental, and physical - are a result of the subconscious trying to let us know that we have unresolved issues that need to be addressed.

And when we finally heal the baggage, and the challenge has served its purpose, it stops. As quickly as my soy intolerance vanished on that fateful day. A machine is truly not necessary.

In fact, it eventually became apparent to me that, while BIE could heal intolerances, it doesn't heal the emotional baggage that created the intolerance in the first place. Consequently, another issue will occur if the original intolerance doesn't return. Having no interest in what I knew was only a "temporary fix," I left BIE to research true, permanent energy healing.

Within just a few months of going "all in" into exploring healing through the subconscious mind, I discovered pendulums, and the world of connections opened up in a way I never expected. With muscle testing, you can receive only three answers: yes, no, and something in-between. A pendulum, however, provides so much more.

I have to thank my sister, Najma, for introducing me to pendulums. She and I were at a family party together, and since I hadn't spoken to her in a while, I was excited to show her how muscle testing could be used to determine whether a person's body "liked" something or not. She politely told me that it was really interesting, but she used a pendulum instead. "What's that?" I asked. In response, she took off her necklace and showed me how, if she held it aloft and asked it to show her "yes," it would move in one direction, and for "no," it would move in another. Before I could fully process what I had just seen, she handed me her necklace and told me to try it.

And by golly, it moved!

She then told me that when she was unsure about a food or something, she would simply ask her pendulum, "is this good for me?" and it would give her an answer. Spying an apple on the table, she handed it to me and told me to ask that question of the apple. Holding the apple in one hand with the necklace hanging over it, I did as she said: I asked "Is this good for me?" And it swung "no". Oh my! I was allergic to apples, and the pendulum moved all on its own to confirm it! I was stunned.

So what exactly *is* a pendulum? And how does it work?

The simplest description of a pendulum is a weight that can swing freely in multiple directions to provide answers to questions. Anything can be a pendulum. A necklace with a heavy pendant. A ring on a string. A fishing lure on some wire. A teabag. A pendulum is a tool, not a special magical device that you can only get in a spiritual shop. I'll describe this in more detail in the next chapter.

As for how it works, the best way I can explain it goes back to my original experience with muscle testing. As said, I see muscle testing as the bridge between the physical and the spiritual.

As you would recall, the "calibration test," where we would test finger strength with the opposite hand on the head, either palm up or palm down, was a tangible way of experiencing energy fields. If we didn't have energy flowing through and around us, with a direction, much like a magnet, hand position would have had no effect.

I, therefore have a way of proving that we have energy fields.

We also discovered that the subconscious can answer yes or no questions by making us stronger or weaker.

It is *shifting our energy* in order to communicate.

Putting the two pieces together, if the subconscious can shift our energy in response to questions, and our energy extends beyond the surface of our skin, then **the energy around us is shifting in response to what our subconscious is projecting**.

I like to refer to a pendulum as an **energy translation device**.

With permission, a pendulum can *tune into one specific person's* (or entity's...more on that in Chapter 11) *energy* and *translate* it into moves that the practitioner can understand. Yes, no, maybe, possibly, probably...a pendulum can communicate all of these and more.

There's a little bit more nuance to it than that (namely, if we're all just broadcasting our energy like our own personal radio station, why does someone need permission to access it?) but bear with me. One thing at a time.

For now, you know what a pendulum is and have a rough idea of how it works. Now, it's time to start getting into the specifics.

Key takeaway:

A pendulum is a tool that allows the user to access information from within the subconscious mind.

CHAPTER 3:
WHAT CAN BE USED AS A PENDULUM?

As I mentioned in the last chapter, any weight on a string can really be used as a pendulum. So before you go out and purchase a pendulum for yourself, it would be a good idea to understand the ins and outs of pendulums first as it may help you narrow down your decision on which one(s) to buy.

In my How to Heal From Your Past online course, I teach my students, quite literally, how to find and heal an event from their past using a pendulum. Most of my students have never even heard of a pendulum before the course, let alone have one on hand to use, so during the second lesson their homework is to find something to use as a pendulum. And no matter what they use, whether it's their favourite necklace, a key hanging on a piece of yarn, or a classic pendulum purchased from a shop, it all works.

It has even happened to me before that I was staying in a hotel room one night, visiting with a friend, when we made an impromptu decision that I would do a healing session for her, only to discover that I had not brought my pendulum with me.

Undaunted, we got a sewing kit from the concierge, and with some thread from the kit, I attached my house key and had a full healing session with it.

And if you've been pregnant, or had a chat with a pregnant woman, there's a good chance you've heard of the "old wives' tale" that you can find out the sex of a baby by dangling a needle on a thread over her belly: if it swings one way, it's a girl, and another way signifies a boy. This is a pendulum! With the moves being predetermined, the subconscious knows what to do to give the desired response. Ask anyone who has tried it, and you'll likely discover how remarkably accurate it is!

While I say anything can be used as a pendulum, I need to clarify a little bit. You can use anything for *dowsing* (i.e., using a tool, such as a pendulum or dowsing rods to **get answers** via the spiritual realm). There are rare circumstances in which using specific pendulums while dowsing may give you better answers. I discuss this in detail in Chapter 13 on what your pendulums should be made of, but (spoiler alert!) if you want to speak to specific guides or entities, *they* may prefer you use a special pendulum, and your answers will come across stronger if you keep them happy. The rest of the time, for dowsing anything will do.

To **shift the energies** needed in *healing* work, you would do well to have a number of different pendulums of various shapes and materials. While it technically can be done with anything you have on hand (as I explained when I did a session using a key on some thread), energy shifts more readily and easily when you have more specific tools. (I refer to my pendulum while healing as my "cosmic vacuum cleaner." Like a vacuum cleaner, any of its attachments would likely get the job done, but if you use the attachment specific for the job, you'll get it done faster and more efficiently.)

For demonstrations of healing work done through a pendulum, you can take a look at the healing demos on my YouTube page: www.YouTube.com/@a.r.t.withrenu

> **Key takeaway:**
>
> *Any handheld weight, suspended so it may swing freely, can be used as a pendulum.*

CHAPTER 4:
WHY WOULD YOU WANT TO USE A PENDULUM, ANYWAY?

What is the use of a pendulum?

Baby gender aside, pendulums are typically used to answer "yes and no" questions, with one swing signifying yes, and another signifying no. Still, other moves may be programmed in to provide alternative responses when more nuance is required, and a simple yes or no may be misleading.

The subconscious mind is the storehouse of all our experiences. It is essentially a computer database. Like a computer, we should always receive an output if we give it input. If we ask a specific enough question about our own past history, we should always get an answer.

Our Higher Self is the Divine part of us whose job is to guide us on our journey; we should be connected to our inner knowing. We should feel confident that we are going in the right direction.

Except that these things don't always happen.

Sometimes there are too many thoughts racing around in our heads, and asking a question doesn't just get a single answer, it gets a cacophony of noise instead.

To put it most accurately, a pendulum is a tool that allows us to sort through the clutter in our minds to get the answers we are looking for.

When trying to explain the human mind, it's helpful to remember one thing: the part of us that sets goals, analyzes situations, asks questions, and makes decisions is the conscious mind—the "I." Everything else—the parts that react to situations, get caught up in negative emotions or self-talk, or even answer the questions we ask ourselves—are all part of the subconscious. Not only that, but it could also include the influence of spirit guides, energies, and other entities. There is so much out there vying for our attention!

When attempting to make a decision, trying to connect to our inner knowing, our divine self, it can be far too "noisy" to hear the true wisdom that lies within us. The multitude of voices in our head - many of them unhelpful! - Leave us uncertain and confused when, in truth, the answers we seek are there, but they are just too quiet compared to the rest of the din.

When we are unable to quiet our minds or are simply not attuned to the method by which our intuition has been trying to communicate with us, a pendulum can be used as a direct line of communication to our inner guidance system; a radio moving through the static to tune into the one channel we want to listen to.

And then there's the healing.

Mental, emotional, spiritual, and even physical issues are all just manifestations of energy trapped within our bodies. The issue is no longer manifested when all the trapped energy is released.

Pendulums are powerful tools for shifting this energy, whether removing or bringing in positive energy. The only catch is that you need to know specifically what energy needs to be shifted, and hundreds of energy types could be stuck at the root of an issue. (An emotion? A belief? A curse? A karmic contract? A past life event? The list goes on and on.) That said, with resources that can help you identify specific energy types, and the knowledge of how to use your pendulum to shift them, you have the tools to bring about happiness, ease, and flow into your life.

While I will be sharing with you some insight into pendulum healing in Chapter 16, most of my tools are outside the scope of this book. Much more is possible using the Accelerated Release Technique™ (A.R.T.). For more information visit the A.R.T. website at www.acceleratedreleasetechnique.org

Key takeaway:

Pendulums are used to facilitate decision-making by bypassing the "mental noise," and to heal energies trapped within the subconscious.

CHAPTER 5:
THE BODY PENDULUM

No discussion of pendulums would be complete without a description of the "body pendulum," also known as the "sway test." If you don't have a pendulum on hand and you're uncomfortable with muscle testing yourself, your own body can also be used to get answers!

While you will be able to program your pendulum with specific yes and no answers, when it comes to the body pendulum, you will have to let your body decide for you what the answers will look like. The first step is to stand up and ground yourself, taking a few deep breaths. Make sure your feet are firmly planted on the ground and you feel secure.

Ask your body to show you a "yes" response and then wait. Within a few moments, you will feel your body sway in one direction or another. Most common is the sensation of being pulled forward, but you may sway backward, or towards one side or the other.

Now you know how your body says yes.

Next, you will ground yourself again and ask your body to show you what a "no" response looks like. Most often, this leads to a feeling of being pulled backward, but any of those other motions is also possible.

You've now got your "no" answer and are ready to get answers from your subconscious.

With that, you can start asking questions and allow your body to give you the answers.

I have also seen unexpected body responses. In my very first class, one of my students, when checking for her "yes" response, didn't feel her body move at all; instead she felt her hands start to get very hot. Then, when it was time to get a "no" response, they turned icy cold.

I'll have to admit, the entire class was jealous. Imagine you are in the grocery store, and you want your subconscious to tell you if that cantaloupe is ripe. It's much less conspicuous for your hands to turn hot than to have to stop in the aisle to check if you start to sway forward!

Key takeaway:

Your body can be used to get answers just like a pendulum!

CHAPTER 6:
HOW TO USE A PENDULUM

You've got your pendulum. You know what you might want to use it for. Now let's get into the practical elements of using a pendulum.

There is nothing mystical about how to use a pendulum, although there are some practicalities to consider that may make it easier.

Hold the pendulum in your dominant hand. With time and practice, your fingers will be able to sense the pendulum motions more than your eyes, so you will find your dominant hand more suitable to the task.

Many dowsers will tell you to grasp the loop or ball at the top of the chain and let it dangle from your thumb and index finger. While this is not technically incorrect, this grip will prevent you from sensing the pendulum motions I described above, and will keep you reliant on purely visual cues to know what answers are being received.

I strongly recommend you hold the chain in such a way that it will slide or rub against your fingers as it moves. Personally, I grasp the pendulum by the chain, immediately beneath the tip, between the pad of my thumb and the side of my index finger, lightly enough that I can feel the chain moving between my fingers. Only by having this contact with the chain will you begin to sense changes in movement even before you see the shift in direction.

You will also need to pay attention to how you are holding your arm while the pendulum is swinging. You'll want to hold the pendulum so that it can swing freely while it is in your hand, so it is best to keep your elbows up with your forearm parallel to the ground or table. In this position, whether the pendulum is moving front-to-back, side-to-side, in circles, or in any other direction, it should not bump into your own arm as it moves.

In time, once you find that your fingers are sensing the pendulum's motions, and you can reliably predict how the pendulum is about to swing, you won't need to be so worried about keeping your elbows up at all times because a simple move of the wrist can keep the pendulum from swinging into you.

bit.ly/HoldPendulum

Now that you're holding your pendulum correctly, all you need to do is ask a yes-or-no question and allow the pendulum to move freely in response. That's it.

Start off with very simple questions, ones where you know the answer, just so you can see it move of its own accord. For example, I might say, "Is my name Renu?" and wait while it begins to move to a "yes" response. Or I could say, "Is my name George?" and watch it move in the direction of "no."

Once you have got past the initial excitement of realizing that the pendulum is indeed moving on its own (I've never seen anyone yet pick up a pendulum for their first time and not be amazed!) you are ready to start asking questions to which you don't know the answers.

There are guidelines for what questions you should and should not ask your pendulum that I cover in Chapter 12, but right now your task is to get used to asking all of your questions in order to get yes or no as a response. So keep your questions simple as you practice this skill.

While strictly "yes or no" may at first seem limiting, if you can get creative, there's almost nothing you can't get an answer to.

Lists are a fantastic way to get very specific answers using yes or no questions.

For example, if I have a list of things I need to do in a day (or a week!), I'll write them all in a numbered list and then when I'm deciding what I ought to be doing at any given time, I'll rattle off the numbers on the list and go with the one that gives me a yes answer.

Tip: when you've got more than a handful of items to choose from, instead of listing them off one by one, you would do best to "chunk them" down in stages. For example, if I've got 20 things on my list, my first question would be "Should my next task be from numbers 1 to 10? Or 11 to 20?" If I got a no for 1-10, then I've just eliminated half my list with one question, and I know to look in the second half. I could then chunk it down even further and ask, "is it in 11 to 15? Or 16 to 20?" Now, I've narrowed it down to 5 possible answers. At that point, I'll just go through each number individually until I receive a yes.

Since your subconscious knows more than you do, I recommend you add the option of "not on the list" to your list just in case there's a priority item you haven't thought of yet.

And since I'm a bit of a workaholic, I typically include "take a break!" in there, too. ☺

To-do lists are just the tip of the iceberg. Any time you need to make a choice when a bunch of options are available, making a list and using your pendulum is an easy way to make your decision. With your own resource lists, you can use your pendulum to find almost any answer you can imagine!

Aside from resource lists, another option is to use pendulum charts. These are single pages with answers arrayed about in either a full circle or half-circle. To use these, you ask your question while holding your pendulum in the center of the circle, and it will swing in the direction of your answer. A few pendulum charts have also been included in the appendix to this book.

bit.ly/UseResourceLists

If you use your pendulum the way most people will tell you to, holding your hand completely still and stopping your pendulum before asking each question, this would be a *painfully slow* process, and you would very likely give up within just a few minutes.

Lucky for you, you've got this book! My next two chapters are filled with tips and tricks to get answers so quickly that you'll even surprise yourself.

Fun fact: all your pendulum questions can be asked out loud or silently. Everything about you that manifests in the physical realm—including the sounds that form words when they leave your mouth—also exists in an energetic form in the spiritual realm. You don't need to speak out loud for beings that exist purely in spirit to "hear" and respond to you. The same applies when using your pendulum to answer questions for another person: they only need to think of the question, and your pendulum will respond to their thoughts!

Our subconscious mind is such a powerful receiver that it, too, can also pick up energetic signals. This phenomenon is evident during hypnosis sessions when a client is in a deep hypnotic trance. The hypnotist receives answers from them using ideomotor responses (for example, if the client's subconscious wants to answer yes, it might twitch the index finger of one hand, and if it wants to answer no, it might twitch the thumb). In such a case, the hypnotist can ask their questions silently and receive ideomotor replies to those questions, too!

Key takeaways:

First, dowsers who receive answers most quickly do not rely only on sight. Hold your pendulum in such a way that you can feel the chain slide against your fingers as it moves. Eventually you will begin to sense the pendulum changing direction before there is any evidence for your eyes to see.

Second, we receive answers from our pendulums in two main ways: we can either ask "yes and no" questions and have our pendulum respond in predefined motions, or we can have an array of pre-prepared answers, as in a pendulum chart, and ask it to point to the one we are looking for. Pendulum charts are limited to the number of answers that can be arrayed in the circle, so arranging all your possible answers into lists, and then using yes and no questions to yield your answer is a way to make your pendulum vastly more useful.

CHAPTER 7:
HOW TO PROGRAM A PENDULUM

The first thing you'll want to do to get faster answers from your pendulum is to make sure that your "yes" and "no" are NOT clockwise and counterclockwise swings.

There are additional reasons, which I will share later, for avoiding those specific moves, but given that "yes" and "no" are going to be your most common answers, and you want to be able to go from one to the other quickly, there is nothing slower than having them as your two single most diametrically opposed movements. In order to move from a clockwise circular spin to a counterclockwise spin, your pendulum must literally stop before it can change direction. (Imagine a car going from forward to reverse: it cannot do so without stopping first, however brief the stop may be.)

It's possible you may be thinking, "but, those are my pendulum's movements!" I promise you, all is not lost.

When I started with pendulums, I was told that your pendulum will tell you what moves meant what. This is possibly something you yourself have heard at some point. For example, it moved front-to-back when I originally asked it to show me a "yes" answer. It told me a "no" answer was a counter-clockwise swing. And for a long time, that's all I knew.

It's WRONG.

Here's the thing. YOU are in charge. Your pendulum is a tool. It's a weight on a string. I won't deny that you can feel a stronger connection to some pendulums than others, with some of them being more meaningful to you, and therefore working better for you, but that doesn't change the fact that the energy driving your dowsing session is yours.

And what if you have multiple pendulums? I've got one in my office, one in my bedroom, and one in my purse. Am I asking each for their yes and no? Not a chance!

You can program your pendulum. You *should* program your pendulum. Tell it what you want a yes to look like. And what you want a no to look like.

Personally, I recommend doing a front to back for a yes...like nodding your head yes. And a side-to-side for a no. Like shaking it, no. At least in North America, those are pretty standard motions. They may be different where you're from, so do what you're comfortable with. If you ever train with me, I'll *insist* that you program in those movements. When I taught my classes in the early days - before I knew better - you can't imagine how confusing it was for me to try and help my various students when everyone's moves meant something different!

Programming pendulum moves is actually very easy to do, as I describe below. So you don't really have a good excuse not to.

I have other reasons for insisting on these particular moves, beyond just keeping my brain from hurting, which I will describe for you in detail when we start talking about using a pendulum to heal, but this alone is a good enough reason to be honest!

To program "yes":

Begin moving your pendulum from front to back and as you do so, repeat the following phrase twice: "This is a yes. This is an affirmative response. This is a beneficial response."

When you're done, stop your pendulum and ask it to show you a yes. It should swing front-to-back. If it doesn't, repeat the programming until it does.

To program "no":

Begin moving your pendulum from side-to-side and as you do so, repeat the following phrase twice: "This is a no. This is a negative response. This is a non-beneficial response."

When you're done, stop your pendulum and ask it to show you a no. It should swing side-to-side. If it doesn't, repeat the programming until it does.

That's it!

bit.ly/ProgramPendulum

Key takeaway:

> *You can, and should, program your pendulum's movements. Your pendulum is only a tool. YOU are in charge.*

CHAPTER 8:

HOW TO GET ANSWERS THAT ARE BOTH FAST AND ACCURATE

Now that you've got your pendulum moving in directions that will serve you better, pay close attention to the following tips and tricks to get answers more quickly, but with confidence that the answers you get are correct.

1. Pendulums seem to defy physics.

If you watch videos of me using my pendulum, you will see that my hand is constantly in motion. As soon as I sense a change in direction, I'll move my arm in response to maintain the momentum. Why do I do this?

By allowing my hand to follow along with the pendulum's movement, I am giving it more energy to swing. If you've ever played on a swing set as a child, you probably remember how much work it took to initially get a good swing going, but once you had gotten high enough, it was much easier to maintain the motion, right? A pendulum is much the same.

Yes, you can keep your hand still and allow micro-movements to gradually provide enough energy to get the swing going, but that is SO SLOW!! A pendulum moving in great big swings is far easier to read than one that is barely moving at all, so if you can help it along, you'll have a much clearer indication of the pendulum's direction.

Now, you might be worried that moving your hand will influence the direction of the pendulum. I promise you, it doesn't. On the contrary, moving your hand will actually **help you feel more confident in the answers you're receiving.**

Here's why.

When I first started using a pendulum, and before I knew how to program my moves, my "yes" was a front-to-back motion, and my "no" was a counter-clockwise circle. My use of a pendulum requires a LOT of questions, with energy shifting in between. The problem is, energy shifts much slower than you are able to think. What that meant for me is that if I were asking, "is this energy now fully released?" I would often get a yes answer (front-to-back) right away, but if I asked again 10 seconds later, it would switch to a no (counter-clockwise swing). It was so frustrating!

I got to the point of just waiting and asking the question repeatedly, just to be certain that my pendulum wouldn't start doing a slight oval motion, which would gradually widen into the full "no" answer.

The thing is, I'm not always the most patient person in the world, and I figured there had to be a way to get the correct answer more quickly.

With some experimentation, I realized that if I moved my arm side-to-side while my pendulum was moving front-to-back, the extra sideways motion could provide just enough momentum to "kick" my yes answer into a no, but **only** if it was going to shift to a no anyway. If it is truly a yes answer, my arm will feel like it is pushing against an invisible wall, actively keeping the pendulum moving straight. It's an extraordinary feeling!

Before going any further, I want you to stop right now and test this out for yourself. It will only take 10 seconds but will change your belief around pendulums forever. Now that you've programmed your yes to front-to-back, I want you to think of a question with a yes answer. With your pendulum swinging, I want you to allow your hand to slowly move back and forth, going right to left and left to right, opposite to the direction of your pendulum. As long as you are focused on your "yes" answer, you will notice that you will feel some resistance, as though there is a wall of force making sure your pendulum continues to move in a front-to-back direction.

Seriously cool, no?

So the answer is definitely, no, you are NOT affecting your pendulum's answers when you move your hand along while it is in motion, either giving it extra energy or verifying the answer you are receiving. Your pendulum will adjust to ensure you receive the answer you're supposed to.

2. Don't stop your pendulum between questions!

The second reason you want your pendulum to have lots of energy while swinging is because it will also change directions much more quickly.

Nothing is slower than beginning from zero.

In the last chapter, I mentioned that you don't want to have your yes and no responses to consist of the clockwise and counterclockwise swings. There is no "quick" way to shift from one to the other - your pendulum *must* stop in between.

But if your yes is front-to-back and your no is side-to-side, then quickly going from one to the other only requires the pendulum to move around in the other direction. Much like a driver joining a freeway and going westbound when they were originally traveling north. The transition is completed in a heartbeat.

So if you want your pendulum to give you its answers quickly, keep it in motion between questions. Don't stop it.

In fact, *start* with your pendulum moving. There is no reason for your first question to start from zero. What direction? That will be answered in my next tip.

There is only one small issue I have to share with you about following the above tips. I have to admit that my particular technique *does* lead to the regular question of "are you moving the pendulum?" to which I have only one reply: "If I knew the answers ahead of time, I wouldn't need to use the pendulum at all!" So, don't let that concern stop *you* either. :)

bit.ly/KeepPendulumMoving

3. Make your pendulum switch directions

While I suggest you start with your pendulum in motion, the only way to be certain that your pendulum is "answering" you and not merely swinging along with whatever momentum you gave it to begin with, is to frame your question(s) in a way that you force your pendulum to change direction. In some situations, this may require phrasing your questions to yield both a positive and a negative response.

For example, when I'm searching for an answer on a table, I will start my pendulum moving in a "no" motion. As I'm questioning the various rows and columns, I expect most answers to be "no" but when I reach the one I'm looking for, my pendulum will change directions to a yes. The forced directional change gives me confidence that I have landed on the answer I'm looking for, so I don't need to check any further.

However, when I'm looking for answers that are not so straightforward, or where there may be a little more nuance, I'll ask my question in several different ways to confirm the answer I've received.

Let's try something simple: should I attend the party tonight?

First, Is it a good idea to attend the party tonight? And see what answer I get.

Then I would rephrase and ask: Is it a bad idea for me to attend the party tonight?

If it's a good idea, you'll get a yes response to the first question and a no response to the second. If it's a bad idea, you'll get the opposite. Either way, your pendulum will be forced to switch directions, which helps you be more comfortable and get an accurate response.

Let's say your first answer was yes, but you had started your pendulum moving in a yes direction. You could restart your pendulum in a no motion and then ask your question again. If it switches to yes, you can feel confident that you have the answer you were meant to receive.

bit.ly/PendulumDirectionSwitches

4. Keep in mind that the subconscious is pedantic

When you ask a question with only yes or no as an answer, majority rules.

That is to say, if you ask a question where the answer isn't black or white, a *mostly* true answer will elicit a yes response.

Going back to the question of going to a party, our assumption was you only had two choices: go to the party or not. Let's say your subconscious said yes, it's a good idea to go to the party.

Well, between going and not going, did not going mean staying home? Or going someplace *else*?

If you were only considering staying at home, then between the two, maybe going to the party was the better alternative for your personal happiness.

But maybe there was a third option that you hadn't considered. And by asking other questions, or *better*, questions, your subconscious would reveal it to you.

Possibly questions like:

Is it in my best interest to go to the party tonight?

Would it be in my best interest to stay home tonight?

Is there something else I would enjoy more than the party?

There is a single rule for working with a pendulum which I have learned over the years: *Ask a better question, get a better answer.*

So play around with your questions! I'm often surprised when I decide to throw in another question or phrase it in a different way, and it reveals something I wasn't expecting. The inner workings of the subconscious are complex, and it is only through learning to ask good questions that we may begin to understand it.

Key takeaways:

To get answers both quickly and accurately, you must first trust that your actions will not accidentally force your pendulum into giving you incorrect answers. Keeping your pendulum in motion leads to getting answers more quickly. Asking your questions in various ways and forcing your pendulum to change directions to confirm answers are the ways to be certain your answers will be as accurate as possible.

CHAPTER 9:
PENDULUMS CAN ANSWER MORE THAN YES AND NO

So far, you've got a yes and a no answer for your pendulum. There's no reason to stop there. When using muscle testing before my introduction to pendulums, I could get only 3 answers…yes, no, and something between a yes and no. That's it. With a pendulum, I discovered that you can get so many other answers that a whole new world opened up!

The thing about not being taught, however, is that I had to stumble through each new discovery.

Over time, and on several occasions, I would be in the middle of a session with someone, and my pendulum would start moving in a brand new pattern and I would be flummoxed as to what it was trying to tell me. I'd ask for every meaning I could think of until it would finally move "yes" to indicate that I had come up with the correct answer. In this way diagonal moves – "maybe" and "possibly" and the clockwise circle "I don't wish to say" all popped up.

Later, my pendulum would make an intricate counter-clockwise flower pattern, providing me with the most useful pendulum move in my arsenal: "You're on the right track."

You wouldn't believe what a helpful move it is! Especially in my work, where I help people connect their problems or challenges to the emotional baggage at the root, my clients and I are constantly playing detective, working together to zero in on key life events from their past. For example, let's say I've been able to give them some information on their event, and they say – oh! Was it that time with my brother at the mall? And I get "you're on the right track". It really means you're *partly* correct. They really gave me two pieces of information... brother, and mall. What if their brother was involved, but not at the mall. Or it was at the mall, but not with the brother. A yes answer is obviously incorrect, but a no answer would be throwing out key information. On the right track allows more nuance so we can more quickly get to the answer we're looking for.

Now, in addition to yes and no, you can program in your own useful moves, like maybe, possibly, unclear, or can't answer, or try again later. Whatever speaks to you. Program them in the same way we did for yes and no. (Before you begin programming all your new moves, read my next chapter on pro-tips for programming your pendulum. Then, by all means, have at it!)

One of the more interesting techniques in my arsenal came about while I was working with a client who had DID—dissociative identity disorder (formerly known as multiple personality disorder). My pendulum began tracing a partial flower pattern, moving back and forth within just one quarter of a circle. It turned out to be an interruption! One of my client's other personalities wanted to come through and speak to us. They used that movement to signal that they wanted our attention. Later, that same pattern emerged with other clients when one of their spirit guides wanted to get our attention to deliver a message during the session!

One of my funniest pendulum move stories actually happened to one of my students, whom I will call Jane. It speaks volumes about the power of the subconscious mind.

Jane was at home using her pendulum, asking it various questions and generally having fun getting answers. After one question, however, it wouldn't give her a yes or no answer, but instead moved about in some strange pattern. Repeating her question kept giving her that same response. She asked her subconscious every possible meaning for that move that she could come up with, but for each suggestion she was given, no, that's not it.

She finally gave up and resolved that she would simply draw the pattern out and then ask me and my then-partner if we could make any sense out of it.

However, she realized that the image looked strangely familiar once she saw it drawn out in front of her.

It was exactly like one of her rune stones...

She immediately went to look up the meaning of that rune and discovered that it was the answer to the question she had been asking!

How cool is that??

The subconscious wants you to get the answers to your questions. And because Jane was so familiar with her rune stones, it knew it could lead her to a better answer the way it did.

So the next time you get a crazy move in response to a question, get creative, too! Draw it out. Or ask your pendulum if it's trying to point you to a resource you have in your home that might get you an answer that's better than a simple yes or no. The answers are all inside you. Trust that you'll be able to find them.

Key takeaway:

Pendulums can answer more than yes and no. The answers you may receive are limited only by your creativity to program in different moves for your subconscious to communicate with you.

CHAPTER 10:
PRO-TIP FOR PROGRAMMING YOUR PENDULUM

As I have said before, all of my original pendulum moves were developed as a result of my pendulum (subconscious!) being in charge and telling *me* what meant what.

Only after several years did I learn that a pendulum is a tool responding to your subconscious, not the other way around. It was a course in something called "Transcendental Dowsing" that taught me that it was possible to program (or re-program) our pendulum to move in the ways we ask it to for the various answers we would like to receive.

That same course also revealed to me that certain pendulum moves are universal to some of the more powerful, energetic experiences. The first one is the counterclockwise circle. It was said that in nature, counterclockwise motions accompany destruction, removal, or cleansing – think of tornadoes, hurricanes, or cyclones. Conversely, clockwise patterns in nature are seen representing growth, as in seashells or the Fibonacci sequence. These are therefore, moves that are reserved for releasing negative stuck energies and anchoring positive ones. These moves can be used to shift energy.

So, if you intend to do healing work with your pendulum, I suggest you reserve the clockwise and counterclockwise moves for healing activities only.

This is why, not just for the sake of consistency, I ask practitioners of my healing modality, the Accelerated Release Technique™, to use a front-to-back pendulum motion to represent "yes" and a side-to-side swing to represent "no." I leave it to the individual practitioner to program all the other motions as they wish, as long as they avoid using circular swings for those other moves. Diagonals, figure eights, even staying still...there are plenty of other creative motions will suffice.

Now you've got all the mechanics of pendulums down - what they are, and how to program and use them, but don't put this book away and dive in just yet. You should be aware that you now have access to a tool that can be used to connect with *all* of the spirits and souls that exist within the Universe, and they're not all nice. They are not all friendly, And some of them might even attempt to actively sabotage you. The first thing to do is be aware of them. Then we'll discuss what to do about them.

Key takeaway:

If you intend to do any healing work with your pendulum, reserve the clockwise and counterclockwise pendulum moves for that.

CHAPTER 11:
CONNECTING WITH... WHAT?

Your pendulum is poised and ready to ask questions and get answers.

But...from where? Or from whom?

I had wanted to title this chapter as "Connecting with the Subconscious," but that gave me pause. It's too limiting. You see, when we connect to our subconscious mind, we are connecting to that piece of ourselves that is wholly intertwined with Universal Consciousness. You cannot connect to the one without being open to the other.

The best way I have to express this is that while you are using your pendulum to get answers, it is akin to making a telephone call to your family home and being put on speaker phone. You may ask to speak to one specific person, but you never really know who is listening, and (since you can't distinguish "voices" with a pendulum) you can't be certain that someone else didn't interject an answer.

When your soul took up a body in this lifetime to have an earth experience, you didn't do it alone: your Higher Self is there to guide you on your spiritual path; your Spirit Guides are there to provide you with support and assistance as you journey through life; your Inner Child exists to preserve your sense of fun, the drive to explore, and your childlike wonder, for all your days; and there's your Ego, too, whose job is to help shelter you from unpleasant experiences so you can pick up and keep going.

None of us could function without them. But you must understand that none of them is YOU. They all have a separate consciousness. You can converse with any or all of them.

And unfortunately, your Spirit Guides, your Inner Child, and your Ego, can all be affected by trauma, just as you can.

Your Spirit Guides are your ancestors—parents, grandparents, and so on—as well as deceased friends and loved ones from this lifetime. They are the people who make up your "soul tribe." You are all on this earthly journey together, learning, growing, and evolving as a group. Your Spirit Guides are just like you, but they are between reincarnation cycles and currently exist without physical bodies. They live entirely in spirit form. Whatever they learn in life, they carry into their next lifetime. This means they don't suddenly become "enlightened" after death; they retain all the emotional baggage in spirit that they had in life.

The result? It is entirely possible for them to allow their trauma to interfere with your life, leading to emotional, mental, spiritual, or even physical problems for you to struggle with as a result. And with the answers you get while using your pendulum!

Your Inner Child holds onto the trauma of your younger self. They, too, may be uncomfortable with your line of questioning and get in the way of receiving clear answers as well.

And your Ego? Its entire job is to protect you. If you start asking questions where it believes knowing the truth will cause discomfort, it can also shut down the conversation.

There is no guarantee that you can receive answers from Angels or God/Divine themselves using a pendulum because of the potential for interference.

This is not to say that a pendulum isn't useful to talk to them - far from it! You just need to be wary of what you ask with your pendulum because of the potential for interference from your otherwise well-meaning support team.

You would do well to lay the "ground rules" before you start a conversation with your guidance team. You will find a protective invocation in Chapter 18: A pendulum session – start to finish. (You'll need the information from a couple more chapters before you will be able to invoke it, so I'm not including it here right now.) The purpose is to minimize interference, or, at the very least, to know before you begin to not waste your time if you receive that any part of your team is uncomfortable with the line of questioning you are contemplating, as you would only receive false or misleading answers.

Once you have established exactly with whom you would like to connect and have done what you can to minimize interference, you're ready to get some answers. In the next chapter, we'll cover what kinds of questions to ask and what not to ask.

Key takeaway:

When using a pendulum, one cannot guarantee a private conversation that is free from interference. If we are not aware of this, we leave ourselves open to the many spiritual beings who may try to influence the answers we receive.

CHAPTER 12:
WHAT TO ASK, AND NOT TO ASK

There is a nearly unlimited number of questions you may ask.

Should I wear this? Or that? Will this food be okay for me to eat? Will this supplement help me? Should I take one pill? Two? Do my plants need watering right now? Which of these items on my to-do list should I tackle first? I could go on and on *and on*!

The most important thing to remember, however, is to not ask any questions in which you have a vested interest in the answer. If you'd like to ask a question and strongly desire a particular outcome, STOP. We have so many protecting influences around us (enough for me to teach several lessons on) that some number of them will undoubtedly interfere so we don't feel the hurt or disappointment in the moment from the answer we receive. It could be our own Ego, spirit guides, or any number of outside energies getting in the way of the truth. And it only takes one to do it.

As I mentioned in the last chapter, while you may only be interested in hearing from one particular spiritual being, using a pendulum opens a channel in which any one spirit can "hijack" the conversation at any time because *they don't want to go there,* either out of a desire to protect you, or to protect themselves.

The only defense against this (unless you have the pendulum healing skills that can counteract the interference) is to stick to questions where you have no bias towards the answer. You must be open to whatever response you receive, because to do otherwise would leave you susceptible to hurt or disappointment, which is exactly what your Ego and other protectors are eager to have you avoid.

So, it is truly vital that you only ask questions where you are indifferent to the response you hear. Where you don't need to be "protected" from the answer.

There are a couple of different answers we may be protected from. We could be protected from things we don't really want to know (e.g., "Will Dad survive his stroke?") and from things we don't want to deal with (e.g., "What experience caused my fear of heights?").

For the first type, I suggest you don't even bother with things where you want to hear a certain answer. It's a recipe for heartache and disappointment. *And* for losing trust in your dowsing when you feel like it "lied" to you.

It's when it comes to encountering things that you would rather not deal with, because they may bring up painful emotions, that it gets interesting!

This is one of the biggest challenges in healing our emotional baggage. It's unpleasant. It's uncomfortable. It's not fun to think about. So your Ego, your Inner Child, or other energetic influences may block the information from coming out. What's really going on is that those same influences themselves need healing so that *they* are not triggered by uncovering the experiences. In truth, they are protecting themselves. Once they feel better, they no longer get in the way, and the emotional trauma becomes available to heal.

While deep healing is outside of the scope of this book, in my chapter on healing with a pendulum, I share some tools on how to get past some of those energies/entities so you can accomplish more with your pendulum than you might have been able to otherwise.

If you have been contemplating using a pendulum for any kind of energy work or connecting with particular spiritual beings, you'll need to move past simple household items and invest in some special pendulums for these tasks. So let's shift gears now and discuss buying pendulums.

Key takeaway:

Only ask questions where you feel detached from the answer, avoiding questions where you have a preference for a particular response. There are too many protecting influences that will seek to avoid disappointing us now irrespective of the disappointment we may feel later from having received false answers.

CHAPTER 13:

DOES IT MATTER WHAT YOUR PENDULUM IS MADE OF?

The answer really depends on what you're planning to do with it.

When it comes to dowsing, my answers come a little bit from picking up pendulum lore, a little bit from scientific understanding, and a little bit from checking in with my own Higher Self.

When I was first introduced to pendulums, my mentor impressed upon me that I should use metal pendulums over crystal ones because metals are natural conductors of energy and "crystals have their own energy that may influence the answers you receive." The only exception to the rule, she said, were clear quartz crystals which "amplify energy rather than hold onto it." (This makes sense if you think of the clear quartz used in watches and other electronic devices.)

Consequently, for most of my career, I have only used metal pendulums to dowse for answers and have been using the same few pendulums for nearly a decade. The only time I've used anything other than my usual 3 pendulums (one which I keep in my office, a second in my bedroom, and the third in my purse) was during the trip I've mentioned previously where I didn't have a pendulum on hand and used a key on a piece of thread instead.

This means I have never personally challenged this assertion and cannot say for certain that you would be better off exchanging that beautiful amethyst or rose quartz piece for something made of steel or brass.

What I can say, though, is that objects certainly can hold onto energy. They can absorb negative energy from the goings-on around them, sometimes enough that they will feel "icky" or uncomfortable to touch.

I recently had a client remark on just this phenomenon with a watch he had recently purchased. He had been eying the watch for some time before buying it, but whenever he would put it on, he felt a heaviness in his body - in his head and chest - with a distinctly "wrong" feeling that would disappear as soon as he took it off.

It took a little work, but I was eventually able to shift the energy so that he could wear the watch without the heaviness that had accompanied it before.

Does this happen to metal objects, too? Or just less frequently? I don't know. I would say that if something was wrong with your pendulum, you would very likely sense it, and then could use a second pendulum (or a key on a string!) to shift the energy around the first.

So, comparatively speaking, it is definitely true that metal does not pick up much energy while other materials do, requiring that they be cleansed on a regular basis. Metal is a conductor. As such, it doesn't hold onto its own energy (or pick up much energy from you or anyone else who uses it), so if taking special care of your pendulum is not high on your priority list, then best to stick with metal. (In Chapter 16, I'll share with you how you can clean your pendulum in a matter of seconds, so that may change your mind.)

In a previous chapter, I discussed who (or what?) you may be connecting with when you pick up your pendulum to get answers to your questions. Suffice it to say, there are many spiritual beings out there whom we may connect with, and depending on who you want to speak to, you may wish to use a different pendulum, because *they* may have a preference. And if you're trying to get answers from someone, it can't hurt to appeal to their sense of aesthetics!

For example, the vast majority of the time, I get answers from my subconscious mind. Now, the subconscious mind is like a database - a computer - and as such, it doesn't have its own "personality" or sensibilities that I need concern myself with. Put another way, my subconscious mind doesn't have any preference over which pendulum I use to communicate with it. Therefore, for subconscious work, I recommend metal almost exclusively.

If you are communicating with your Higher Self, I suggest going with the pendulum type - material and shape included - that feels good to you - to encourage freer communication.

Personally, my Higher Self is fine with my metal pendulum. That said, when asking my Inner Child her preference, I got the answer that her favourite is my bloodstone pendulum. Therefore, when I have reason to communicate directly, and I want to use a pendulum to do so, I'll use my bloodstone.

You may also want to use different pendulums to communicate with specific spirit guides - it's possible that they may have their own particular tastes, and you'll get answers more readily using what they prefer.

The divinities - angels/archangels/God/Divine/Source (pick your terminology) don't seem to have a preference that I have seen, rather, they just want you to communicate with them however you do it!

As I mentioned previously, using pendulums for healing, however, is different story entirely. I have a range of pendulums - different metals, different crystals, and wood, all of various shapes - and depending on the task at hand, I may be directed to use one pendulum or another (and sometimes two spinning at once!) I can't say I've figured out a pattern for what gets used when, though. I just go along as I'm directed. ☺

Key takeaway:

For dowsing, you can use any pendulum you like. For healing or communicating with particular spirits/entities, using special pendulums may enhance your experience.

CHAPTER 14:
BUYING A PENDULUM

Once you feel comfortable with the idea of a pendulum - maybe to get answers to your questions, or for healing, or connecting with particular spiritual beings - it's time to consider trading out your key hanging on a string (or whatever household items you've been using) for a conventional pendulum.

While a pendulum *is* just a tool, energetically, you want to make sure that it is the right "fit." Energy will need to flow freely from you and through it; therefore, the most effective pendulums feel like a second skin to wear, like the perfect pair of shoes or gloves.

You need to be comfortable with it. You'll want to like its look and feel. The weight in your hand. It needs to feel like something you want to use. If you don't like the look or feel; if something about using it annoys or irritates you, you won't feel comfortable using it and you will struggle to get easy answers.

Be forewarned, though, the choices can be overwhelming! So how do you choose?

When I got my first pendulum, I was in a store with dozens of them to choose from. How do you pick? If none of them just jump out at you, then here is a trick you can use:

Pick a pendulum - it doesn't matter which one. Since you have been working with pendulums for a long time, and your subconscious knows what to show you for yes and no, simply verify with this new pendulum your yes and no moves. Now you've got a pendulum you can - at least temporarily - work with.

Your first question may be "are you the best pendulum for me?" If you get a yes - great! That was easy. If you get a no, ask yes or no questions to identify the one in the store that is best for you. Before you start, you may even want to check: is there a great pendulum for me in this store? If you get an affirmative answer, you can narrow it down however you see fit. Is it on this rack? In the first display case? In the second row? Etc. Once you identify the "right" pendulum, check your yes and no with it and verify you have the right one.

There are other questions you might want to ask, too. If you wanted your pendulum for a specific purpose, verify that the pendulum you have selected (or are being guided to) will serve that purpose. Your subconscious - or your inner child, or spirit guide etc. - may have its own reasons to encourage you to pick up another pendulum, either in addition to or instead of the one you want. That "great pendulum for me" may be great for a different purpose than we had intended!

Remember, better questions = better answers. As long as nobody is trying to protect you or themselves, you won't be lied to, but since pendulums can only give yes or no answers, lack of specificity in our questions can easily result in us being misled.

A final piece of advice on selecting a pendulum. If you're brand new to working with pendulums and have a few to choose from, then you may want to look for one with a slightly heavy weight as opposed to a very light one, because you'll want to be able to really *feel* your pendulum as it's moving, not just watch it. Also, try to choose one whose chain is not especially long. While you can always keep the chain shorter or longer based on how you grip your pendulum, a very long chain is much more unwieldy and is not recommended. In the beginning, most new users will find that their pendulum moves slowly and tentatively (although, if you follow my advice, this phase should be short-lived!) That said, as you get more experienced and your pendulum moves faster and more forcefully, you'll want to switch to a lighter pendulum. Even the most experienced pendulum users, myself included, will occasionally lose their grip when the pendulum is spinning, and the force from a very heavy pendulum flying across the room might do some damage to yourself or something else!

Key takeaway:

"Outsource" your decision on which pendulum to buy! Pick up any pendulum in the store, verify your yes and no moves, and then use it to help you determine which pendulum(s) to purchase.

CHAPTER 15:
ACCLIMATING TO YOUR PENDULUM

Many people will tell you that for the first few days following the acquisition of a new pendulum, you should keep it as close to your body as possible. Keep it in a pocket (many ladies will keep it in their bra) and sleep with it under their pillow or tucked into their pillowcase. I have witnessed this help some individuals establish a greater connection to their pendulum when it had been lacking, so this is not a *bad* idea. I do, however, take issue with the assertion that it is to attune the pendulum to your energy. Please remember, the pendulum is a tool. Yes, your pendulum could be holding onto some negative energy that needs to be cleansed, which we will be covering in the next chapter, but no, you are not attuning **it to you**. More accurately, you are attuning **yourself to it**.

Like I said in the last chapter, energetically, you want it to feel familiar to you. Answers are going to flow through you to it. You need to feel comfortable with it, not the other way around. (Like breaking in a new pair of shoes.) More often than not, when I have a student who is having difficulty getting their pendulum to move, it is <u>their</u> energy that is blocked, and once we remove the block, the pendulum works fine. Their connection to the pendulum was never the issue.

Personally, upon purchasing my very first pendulum, I did "all the things" I was told to do by my mentor at the time. The bra, the pillowcase, and so on. After that pendulum broke and was replaced, I felt no need to acclimate to the second (or any I bought afterward). By then, I was very comfortable with pendulums and could pick up any weight on a string and use it in a pinch. Treat your pendulum with respect (as you should all of your possessions), but once you anthropomorphize it, giving it a will and personality of its own, you are opening yourself up to the belief that you are not in charge of your own destiny; nothing good ever comes out of holding onto that belief.

And just as you wouldn't think twice about letting someone else handle a hammer or chisel from your toolbox, remember that **your pendulum is a tool, too!** By all means, feel free to cleanse your pendulum after someone else uses it, because they can definitely leave their own energetic residue on it. But, since cleaning it is almost as easy to do as breathing, as I'll describe next chapter, there is no need to make a big deal out of it.

That said, I have no judgment if you don't want to loan your pendulum to someone for other reasons. Like your favourite necklace or watch, it may feel too personal to want to let someone else use, and I get that. Just as long as you recognize that there is nothing inherently wrong about sharing your pendulum. It's a pendulum, not a toothbrush, and it can be cleaned up in seconds.

Key takeaway:

Acclimating to your pendulum is about feeling comfortable with it. There is nothing inherently wrong with keeping your pendulum near you or on your person to "get used to it," but if you feel comfortable from the beginning, there is no need to go through any particular ritual to "acclimatize" to it.

CHAPTER 16:
HEALING WITH A PENDULUM

Even if you do not want to become an "energy healer," I strongly recommend you learn the basics of how to shift energy (aka heal) with a pendulum.

Why? Two reasons.

First, it won't take you very long to exhaust all the "neutral" questions you want to ask your Higher Self. Should I do this or that? Buy this or the other? Eat this? Avoid that? This is all surface-level connection to your intuition. It is a wonderful way to effectively "outsource" your decision-making. (As I described earlier, I love asking my Guidance team to plan my day for me. I provide a list of things I would like to get done, including things like "take a break" and "something not on the list" and ask my team what I should be doing at any given time. I'm now experiencing more work-life balance and not feeling guilty that my never-ending to-do list doesn't seem to be shrinking. I'm allowing myself to give into Divine timing, which is fantastically freeing.)

That said, life is about so much more than simply making decisions. It's about acting on them, too.

And that's where things get challenging.

You can *decide* to exercise, eat better, give up drinking, forgive your ex, become a better public speaker, overcome your fear of heights, or any number of countless examples of things you might want to do.

But as they say, easier said than done.

If it was easy, you probably would have done it by now.

And if it's not easy, there's a reason.

And the reason lies with some programming that currently exists somewhere in your subconscious mind.

If you are able to use a pendulum, you are 90% of the way to being able to rewrite the programming.

In this chapter, I'm going to share with you the basics of how it is done.

And the second reason? Because I've already shared that if you want to get answers via a pendulum, you are at the mercy of your Guidance team to not interfere. If they are interfering, it's only because they are dealing with their own emotional baggage that needs healing. If you know the basics of how to heal *them*, you'll find your pendulum to be useful for much more than you would have otherwise.

Shifting energy with a Pendulum

As I have already shared with you, pendulums can be used for more than dowsing. They can be used to shift energy as well. This is another way of saying they can be used for healing.

I also mentioned that the magic exists in the clockwise and counterclockwise spins.

Clockwise and counterclockwise motions are extremely powerful moves in the world of energy. I refer to it as turning on my cosmic vacuum cleaner.

And just as a vacuum cleaner has multiple attachments, you can shift different energy types depending on how you modify those clockwise or counterclockwise motions.

Modifications can include things like the swing pattern you're using – it could be a gentle circle, a fast circle, a flower pattern or more. You could also have to spin the pendulum over something, like a crystal or a tensor ring. Or maybe you need a particular pendulum of a different shape or made with a different material.

Cleansing objects or spaces

The very simplest one is a gentle counterclockwise spin. You can literally use it to clean the rooms in your house, or specific objects, like your crystals. Simply hold your pendulum over the thing you want to clean (or if it's a room, hold the intention of cleansing the room in your mind) and allow your pendulum to swing counterclockwise until it stops on its own.

If you want to charge something with positive energy, use a clockwise swing instead, holding your pendulum until it's done.

Healing emotions and beliefs

In addition to using pendulums to cleanse energy, I use pendulums to heal emotions and beliefs as well.

For example, if someone is feeling angry or sad or upset or embarrassed, using the right pendulum move with the right additional modifications acts to siphon off those emotions, leaving that person feeling calm and centered once again.

The simplest way for you to do this is in two parts. First, connect with the negative emotions you are feeling, labeling them as you go, and asking for them to be released. For example "I want to let go of the anger and rage I'm feeling, the betrayal, the sadness..." etc. While your pendulum is moving in a counterclockwise direction. The act of connecting with the emotions allows the Universe to be directed to exactly the energy that needs to be removed. Continue to let the pendulum move until it stops on its own.

Then check in on how you are feeling. If nothing interfered with your subconscious's ability to let the emotions go, they should feel lighter. You may feel the same emotions but less intensely, or you may discover another layer of negative emotions. If there are still some negative emotions left, repeat the above process to release them.

Once the negative emotions are gone, you can repeat the process with the addition of positive emotions. While spinning your pendulum in a clockwise direction, ask for the emotions you would like to feel instead. For example "I would like to feel forgiveness, compassion, and empathy. I would like to feel heard and respected..." etc.

Continue until you are feeling better about the situation at hand.

Healing past trauma

My form of energy healing works to heal past trauma. I use my pendulum along with a bunch of additional resources to connect peoples' current challenges to the events or experiences from their past that are really at the root – the emotional baggage that they have been carrying around that has been sabotaging their lives.

The amazing thing is that the subconscious can't tell the difference between something happening right now and something they are thinking about. So, in the same way that one can use a pendulum to siphon off emotions around the things that are going on right now, if someone thinks about their past trauma and I use the same techniques, I can remove all the negative emotions out of their memory. This means that a pendulum can be used to heal past trauma as well.

I have shared only the basics of shifting energy with you. It can get far more complicated when trying to dislodge emotions and beliefs that are very deeply ingrained (potentially from past lives or karmic entanglements with others). Still, these are nonetheless very powerful energy-healing moves that can go a long way to removing the blocks and resistances around taking action in our daily lives. I encourage you to give them a try!

Key takeaway:

The clockwise and counterclockwise pendulum motions are powerful forces in shifting energy. By connecting to the negative energy or emotions that we want to shift and spinning the pendulum at the same time, negative energy can be siphoned off and be replaced with positive energy instead.

CHAPTER 17:
TAKING CARE OF YOUR PENDULUM

Keeping it energetically clean is the only real "care" needed for your pendulum. I've held off on explaining how to cleanse your pendulum because I wanted to share with you how to heal using a pendulum first.

This is because cleansing your pendulum is literally the act of removing negative energy that may have been attached to it during the process of using it. This is exactly what is done in healing work. Just like our homes manage to gather dust through the daily business of living, energy work leaves a residue, too.

If you do a quick search online, you'll find a myriad number of ways suggested to cleanse/charge your pendulums (or crystals in general).

1. Rinse them in cold running water.
2. Bathe them in moonlight, especially under a full moon, overnight.

3. Expose it to sunlight (early morning or late evening sun) by leaving it on your windowsill for up to 4 hours.
4. Bury it in the earth for 24 hours, allowing Gaia (Mother Nature) to ground the negative energy.
5. Set it in a bowl with crystals known for their ability to absorb negative energy, like selenite, amethyst, or citrine, for 24 hours. (You'll then need to make sure those crystals are themselves cleansed).
6. Smudge your pendulum with sage.
7. Use a sound bowl and allow the sound to bathe it in cleansing energy
8. Send it Reiki healing energy
9. Bury your pendulum in brown rice for 24 hours.
10. Submerge your pendulum in a bed of sea salt for a few hours or overnight.

I'm going to let you in on a little secret. EVERYTHING to do with the world of energy is about INTENTION. It doesn't matter which of the above methods you use (although I would strongly caution you against using sunlight, as it can cause your crystals to fade, and salt can corrode your pendulum, depending on what it is made of,) as long as you are taking *intentional action* to cleanse your pendulum.

The one method you won't find online is the one I'm going to share with you. In fact, I've already shared it with you. Use pendulum healing! Your cosmic vacuum cleaner makes this task very short. (*I'm* certainly not taking the time to bathe my crystals in moonlight or even cleansing them under running water when an easy pendulum move will do the trick.)

You'll need a second pendulum to cleanse your first. Hold the pendulum doing the cleaning over the object being cleansed. Allow your pendulum to swing freely in a counterclockwise direction until it stops spinning and moves into a "yes" motion. Then you're done. You can verify that it is now clean if you would like. (If you only own one pendulum, then create a second one using a key on a piece of string or whatever else you have on hand. It will still work.)

If you would like to charge an object with positive energy, allow the pendulum to move freely in a clockwise direction instead. When that has stopped, you're good to go.

Most crystals will be cleansed in a matter of a few seconds. However, black crystals - such as hematite, onyx, and tourmaline, are what I refer to as "negative energy sponges" and have an extraordinary ability to protect by attracting negative energy into them. If you are carrying around one of those stones, you'll feel more grounded and less anxious as a result, but it is important to cleanse those stones regularly because a sponge can only hold so much before it is full and then it will make you feel worse rather than better. You will find these stones take significantly longer to cleanse (still less than a minute!) but the effort is well worth it.

You'll very likely find that your metal pendulums won't take more than a second to clean if that. Again, that is one of the reasons that I've recommended metal pendulums in the first place. Using this technique to verify if they are clean and/or require cleaning is a great way for you to prove this for yourself.

As for how often you need to cleanse your pendulums or crystals, it really depends on how much you use them. I'd suggest you add it onto the "to-do" list we discussed earlier and let the Universe tell you when it needs to be done.

Key takeaway:

Use your new healing technique from Chapter 16 to cleanse your pendulum in seconds!

CHAPTER 18:
A PENDULUM SESSION - FROM START TO FINISH

As I said in the beginning chapters of this book, the main purpose of using a pendulum is to establish a straight connection to our intuition. To cut through the noise and hear what our Divine Guidance team is trying to tell us.

This should be one of the simplest things in the world. In fact, in a perfect world, we wouldn't need a pendulum because we wouldn't have the chatter in our minds interfering with our own intuitive connection. We should be able to simply ask our question in our mind and hear, feel, or in some way sense the answer right away.

But since we don't all live in this world of perfect intuitive sense, we have a tool, a pendulum, to help us bypass the mental clutter. The only issue is that it opens us up to other energies that may interfere differently- by sending answers according to their own agenda.

So at the beginning of the session, we set ground rules. Others may do this differently, but now that I've given you a few healing moves, you'll have the skills to bypass some of the potential interference and determine off the top if your line of questioning is something that you shouldn't bother with because you won't get straight answers. The following statement is for a session in which you are just looking for general advice/answers:

(With your pendulum spinning counterclockwise)

"I ask to connect with my Guidance Team, my inner child, and unconscious mind. I am asking for a 100% crystalline clear connection, that they will address any clarity issues as they arise and remove unwanted or uninvited energies that may attempt to interfere.

"I also ask to receive only 100% true and accurate answers, given concisely and timely, and that they guide me towards *my* Highest, Best, and Greatest Good."

Allow your pendulum to spin counterclockwise until it finishes and begins to move in a "yes" motion, indicating that any interference that might have been there has been removed, and that everyone is "on board" with your intended line of questioning.

The job of your guidance team is to help you. You are asking, encouraging, and empowering them to do this on your behalf by letting them know that they can assist by making sure that you get clear answers.

That said, if you find that your pendulum stops spinning and shifts to a "no" motion, then one of the groups - your spirit guides, your inner child, or something lurking within your unconscious mind - is not comfortable with whatever questions you are thinking about asking and you can expect there to be interference unless you address their issue first. This will require healing the group in question, which is outside this book's scope but may be learned through courses I teach at www.acceleratedreleasetechnique.org.

When I am doing a *healing* session, I adjust the second part of the invocation slightly, saying "I also ask to receive only 100% true and accurate answers, given in a concise and timely fashion, *for the fastest and most efficient healing possible.*" When a guidance team answers "no" to fast and efficient healing, it is an indication that the root of the problem is something they themselves are uncomfortable with accessing, and I need to work with them first to make them comfortable.

Once you receive that your guidance team is on board with your line of questioning, go ahead and ask what you want to ask.

Remember, if you change topics, you'll need to *verify again* with your guidance team that they are okay with answering questions about this *new topic*. I can't think of the number of times I've started a healing session with the intention of working on multiple issues, only to find myself going in circles mid-session because a spirit guide or their inner child was uncomfortable with one of the later issues I began to work on!

Personally, I'm constantly thanking my guidance team for the help they provide me throughout the session, but if that is not your habit, then my recommendation for you when closing out a session is to thank your guidance team for their assistance.

There's nothing else to it.

To recap:

1. Connect to your guidance team, asking them to clear the way for you to ask questions about a particular topic and verifying that they themselves are "on board."
2. Ask your questions.

3. Thank your team.

Key takeaway:

Anytime you begin a new line of questioning, make sure your guidance team is on board and will not interfere with the accuracy of the answers you receive.

CHAPTER 19:
WHEN YOUR PENDULUM DOES "WEIRD STUFF"

Generally speaking, pendulum problems fall into two broad categories: the pendulum is doing something you don't understand, or your pendulum is not working.

For the first category, what to do is simple: ask your pendulum!

I've already given you several stories of how I learned of different pendulum moves or how students have discovered different ways that their pendulum was trying to communicate with them. Your pendulum **is** communicating with you. It is now up to you to figure out what it is trying to convey.

Asking someone else what your pendulum is saying won't help you. Your subconscious is trying to speak *your* personal language. This is where you will find it even more valuable to program in "you're on the right track." Your subconscious will then be able to let you know if one of your guesses is at least partly correct, and you can refine your line of questioning until you get there. We all think differently, and your subconscious knows how *you* think. Keep at it, and you will get there.

As for the other problem, in which your pendulum isn't working - either not moving at all or giving you deliberately false answers - the fix here is less obvious.

When this happens, most likely, it is your own belief system that is sabotaging you.

We manifest what we believe. Our outer experiences are simply an expression of the deep inner workings of our mind. If you can't get your pendulum to work, 90% of the time it is a reflection of your own inability to trust - whether it be trusting the process, trusting your intuition, or trusting your own capabilities.

The remaining 10% may be external factors, such as your spirit guides distrusting the process, the influence of other people in your life who may disapprove of you using a pendulum, or any possible effects from energies around you.

If spending some time acclimatizing to your pendulum doesn't shift this for you, then I'm afraid there is no simple solution to this problem. This is a sign that some healing is required: either you need to do the deep work to understand what beliefs you may be holding onto that could be manifesting in this self-sabotage, or you may need to reflect on the influences in your life - from people living or dead - who may feel that pendulum use is an activity that you shouldn't be engaging in. The energy will need to shift. If you don't have the tools to shift this, you may need help from a professional energy healer. If you don't already have someone you work with, you can always look for an Accelerated Release Technique™ practitioner for help at www.acceleratedreleasetechnique.org.

Key takeaway:

If you don't understand a move your pendulum is making – ask it! It is your own subconscious speaking to you, after all. If you can't get your pendulum to work, however, then there is energy blockage that needs to shift which may require the services of an energy healer.

CHAPTER 20:
SOME FINAL WORDS

In the previous pages, I've shared with you why and how you might want to use a pendulum. How a pendulum works and what it may be used for. How to take care of it. How to get answers faster and more efficiently. Some of the pitfalls and how to avoid them. And how to use it to shift energy and heal.

I hope you have found the information presented both illuminating and valuable, and are already feeling more confident using a pendulum.

As I'm sure I have made it abundantly clear, I find pendulums to be one of the most remarkable tools that exist, and I'm honestly thrilled for every new person I can help develop some proficiency using them.

We are all gifted with intuitive abilities whose job it is to guide us to people, places, and situations that will allow us to become the best versions of ourselves. Not everyone is so well connected to their intuitive sense as to be able to hear it without some outside help, and that is where a pendulum can bridge the gap.

If you use your pendulum regularly, you'll begin to find that you start to "hear" or "feel" or otherwise somehow begin to sense the answer a split second before your pendulum provides it for you. That is your own intuition getting stronger. Lean into that. Test it. The ultimate goal is to learn to trust our intuitive senses...like the body pendulum, they aren't subject to the influence of outside interferences the way a pendulum can be.

If I have incited some excitement and curiosity in you to see how much you can do with a pendulum, then I will consider this book to be a success. That said, if you would like to take your newfound skills to the next level, moving beyond surface-level questions and answers to effecting permanent, life-changing healing, my courses at www.acceleratedreleasetechnique.org are a great place to begin. It would be an honour to continue teaching you!

Key takeaway:

Everyone has their own intuitive gifts, although some people feel them more strongly than others. Using a pendulum can help you strengthen your gifts if you allow it.

APPENDIX

In this appendix are a few handy tools you may want to use.

The first is my "Clues List." I've used this exact list in my healing practice for over 10 years. By watching a few of the older healing demonstrations on my YouTube channel, or better still, by taking my How to Heal Your Past online course, you'll be walked step-by-step on how to find life events and heal trauma and this clues list will be the most important resource to have on hand. You can even use it when you can't quite put your finger on an emotion that you (or the person you are working on) is feeling when you're using Transcendental Dowsing to help someone feel better, simply ask to be directed to the clue that is closest to it on the list.

To find a particular clue on the list, use the same technique I suggested to figure out what action to take on your numbered "to-do" list. Start by finding the column from A-E and then the row, "chunking down" into rows 1-10, 11-20, 21-30, 31-34, before narrowing down to groups of 5, and then finding the individual clue.

The rest of the appendix consists of various pendulum charts you may want to use, or, knowing what they look like, you can use them as a template to create your own. With a little bit of creativity, you can use your pendulum to get all the answers you are looking for!

Clues list

	Column A	Column B	Column C	Column D	Column E
1	Abandonment	Discontented	Hysteria	Love	Self-Pity
2	Absent-Mindedness	Discouraged	Immobility	Mania	Self-Willed
3	Addiction	Disempowered	Immodest	Meanness	Senility
4	Aggression	Disgusted	Immoral	Mental Isolation	Shame
5	Agitated	Disillusioned	Impatience	Mentally Closed	Shock
6	Agony	Disloyal	Inability to Speak	Mentally Lost	Skeptical
7	Anger	Disrespect	Inadequate	Mentally Oppressed	Solitude
8	Anxiety	Distressed	Inattentive	Mistrust	Sorrow
9	Apathy	Doubt	Inconsiderate	Narcissism	Spiritually Lost
10	Arrogance	Embarrassment	Indecisive	Neurosis	Spiteful
11	Astonishment	Emptiness	Inferiority Complex	Nostalgia	Stinginess
12	Betrayal	Envy	Inflexible	Obsessive	Stress
13	Bewildered	Exhausted	Insanity	Obstinacy	Stubborn
14	Bitterness	Failure	Insecurity	Over-Activity	Substance Abuse
15	Boredom	Fear	Inspire	Over-Confident	Suicidal Thoughts
16	Bullying	Fear of People	Intimacy	Over-Estimation of Self	Superiority Complex
17	Burdened	Frustrated	Intolerance	Painful	Support
18	Cheerless	Fulfilled	Irreconcilable	Panic	Tearful
19	Community	Gloomy	Irritability/Excitability	Passivity	Tension
20	Complete	Greed	Jealousy	Peaceful	Terror
21	Concentration	Grief	Joy	Prideful	Timidity
22	Confusion	Guilt	Joyless	Procrastination	Uncaring
23	Control	Guilty Conscience	Kindness	Qualify	Unenthusiastic
24	Cowardice	Hatred	Kleptomania, Thief	Rage	Unfriendliness
25	Deceit	Heartlessness	Lack of Initiative	Rejected	Unfulfilled
26	Dejected	Helplessness	Laziness	Resentment	Ungenerous
27	Depression	Hesitation	Learning Difficulties	Restlessness	Unreliable
28	Deprived	Hopelessness	Lethargic	Restraint	Unsafe
29	Derision	Hot Temper	Liar, Lies	Rudeness	Unsupportive
30	Despair	Humourlessness	Loneliness	Sadness	Vanity
31	Destructive Thoughts	Hyper Sexual	Longing to Die	Self-conscious	Vindictiveness
32	Disappointed	Hypercritical	Loss of Confidence	Self-Deception	Weariness
33	Disapproval	Hypersensitivity	Loss of Dignity	Self-focused	Withdrawn
34	Disbelief	Hypochondriac	Loss of Innocence	Self-loathing	Worry

Percent Chart

0 10 20 30 40 50 60 70 80 90 100

Alphabet Chart

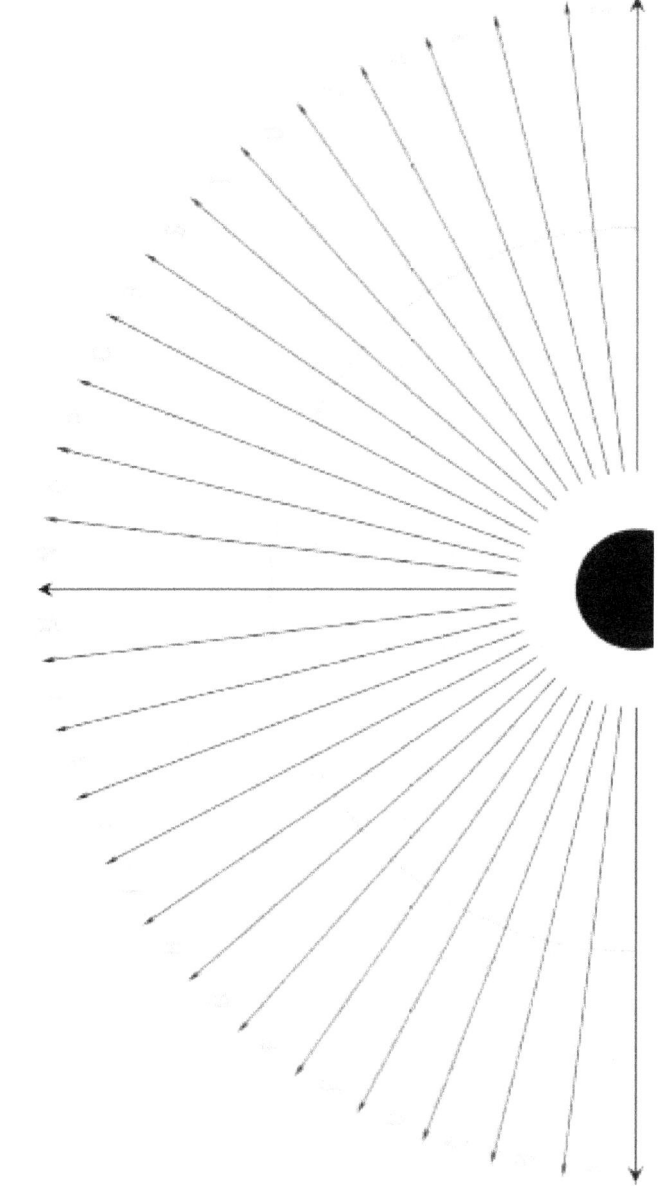

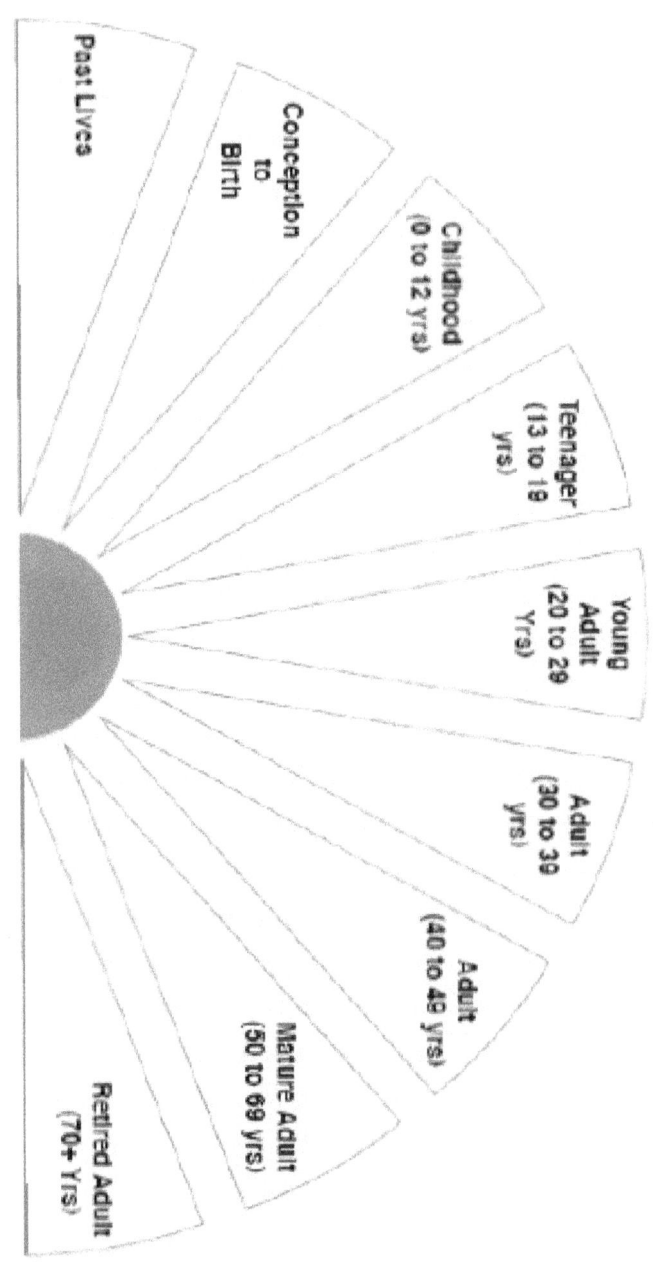

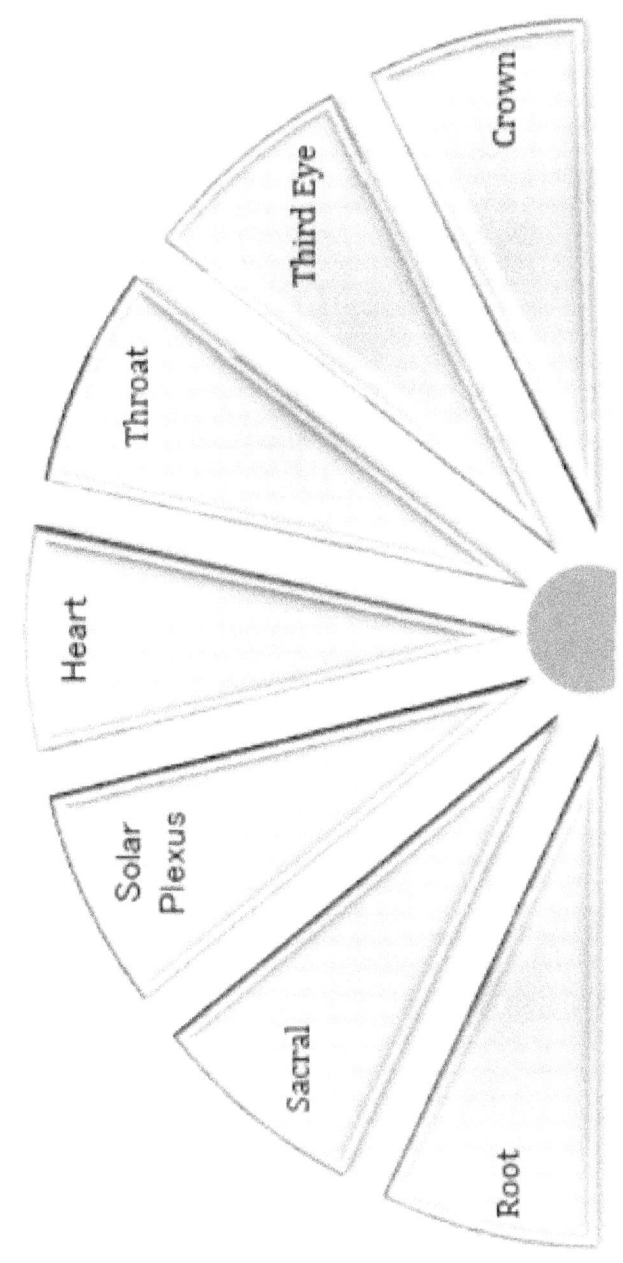

ABOUT THE AUTHOR

Before launching her award-winning career as an energy healer, Renu Arora had received a B.Sc. in biochemistry from McGill University, had already been a Registered Dietitian for over a decade, and was running a private practice in Toronto, Canada.

And then she discovered - first through muscle testing, and later via pendulums - proof that the subconscious can communicate. Not just that, but that it is actively using our current challenges to try to point us to old trauma needing to be healed, and if we do so, our current challenges can go away like magic.

She hasn't looked back since.

Renu can now be found spending most days working with clients, teaching students, or researching energy healing as she continues to improve and refine her healing modality, the Accelerated Release Technique™.

If you would like more information on how you can work with her, visit www.renuarora.ca.

www.ingramcontent.com/pod-product-compliance
Lightning Source LLC
Chambersburg PA
CBHW061338040426
42444CB00011B/2982